PROTEIN PACKED
Salads

50 Delicious and Nutritious Recipes Featuring High-Protein and Moderate-Protein Options

KRUPA AND KRISH

Disclaimer:

The nutritional information provided in this cookbook is intended as a general guideline only. The information is based on the ingredients and quantities used in the recipes, and it does not take into account any variations or substitutions that may be made.

Please note that the nutritional content of a dish can vary depending on the quality and brand of the ingredients used. Therefore, the values provided may not be accurate for your specific situation. We recommend that you consult a qualified nutritionist or dietitian to obtain personalized advice on your dietary needs.

While every effort has been made to ensure the accuracy of the nutritional information in this cookbook, we cannot guarantee that the values are completely error-free. The authors and publishers of this cookbook disclaim any liability or responsibility for any loss or damage that may be incurred as a result of reliance on this information.

Please use your own discretion and judgment when making any changes to your diet or nutritional intake based on the information provided in this cookbook.

We hope that you enjoy the recipes and find them to be a helpful resource for your cooking needs.

Contents

INTRODUCTION

Welcome to "Power-Packed Salads: Fuel Your Day with Flavor and Protein"! In this cookbook, we have curated a collection of 50 mouthwatering salad recipes that not only tantalize your taste buds but also provide a healthy dose of protein to keep you feeling satisfied and energized throughout the day. Our aim is to show you that salads can be both delicious and nutritious, helping you maintain a balanced diet without compromising on flavor.

This book features two distinct sections, offering a wide array of options to cater to diverse dietary needs and preferences. The first section includes 25 recipes that pack a powerful protein punch, with each salad containing over 40 grams of protein per serving. These recipes are perfect for those looking to build muscle, increase energy levels, or simply incorporate more protein into their daily meals.

The second section offers an additional 25 recipes with a moderate protein content of over 25 grams per serving. These salads are ideal for individuals seeking a well-rounded, nutritious meal without an overly high protein intake. They are perfect for maintaining a balanced diet and can easily be tailored to meet specific dietary requirements or preferences.

Throughout this cookbook, you will discover a wide variety of ingredients, flavors, and textures. From leafy greens and hearty grains to succulent fruits and savory proteins, these salads are designed to be as visually appealing as they are delectable. We have included vegan, vegetarian, and meat-based options to ensure there is something for everyone, regardless of dietary preferences.

Each recipe in "Power-Packed Salads" features easy-to-follow instructions, making it simple to create a restaurant-quality salad in the comfort of your own home. We have also included helpful tips and tricks to guide you through the preparation process and ensure your salads are as fresh, flavorful, and nutritious as possible.

So, grab your apron, and let's embark on a culinary adventure that will transform the way you think about salads. With "Power-Packed Salads: Fuel Your Day with Flavor and Protein", you will never have to choose between taste and nutrition again. Enjoy!

ANIMAL BASED HIGH-PROTEIN SOURCES

Chicken Breast: A lean and versatile protein source, chicken breast can be grilled, baked, or pan-seared, making it a popular choice for high-protein salads.

Turkey: Another lean poultry option, turkey is low in fat and high in protein, and can be used in a variety of salad recipes, either ground or in sliced form.

Salmon: Rich in omega-3 fatty acids, salmon is a delicious and nutritious protein source that can be grilled, baked, or pan-seared for a flavorful addition to your salads.

Tuna: Available fresh or canned, tuna is a convenient and protein-packed option that works well in salads, providing a boost of flavor and nutrition.

Shrimp: Low in fat and high in protein, shrimp can be quickly cooked and added to salads for a delicious seafood twist.

Lean Beef: Opt for lean cuts of beef like sirloin or flank steak for a high-protein addition to your salads. Grilled or pan-seared, beef can add depth and flavor to your dishes.

Greek Yogurt: Creamy and tangy, Greek yogurt can be used as a high-protein base for dressings or as a topping to add richness and texture to your salads.

Eggs: Hard-boiled, soft-boiled, or poached, eggs are an affordable and versatile protein source that can be easily incorporated into a variety of salad recipes.

Cottage Cheese: Low in fat and high in protein, cottage cheese can be used as a topping or mixed with other ingredients for a creamy salad base.

Feta Cheese: Crumbled feta cheese adds a tangy, salty flavor to your salads while providing a good amount of protein.

PLANT-BASED HIGH-PROTEIN SOURCES

Lentils: Nutritious and versatile, lentils can be cooked and added to salads for a hearty, protein-packed meal.

Chickpeas: Also known as garbanzo beans, chickpeas can be used in salads whole or mashed, providing a satisfying protein boost.

Black Beans: Rich in fiber and protein, black beans can be added to salads for a flavorful, nutrient-dense option.

Tofu: Made from soybean curd, tofu can be marinated, grilled, or pan-seared to add a high-protein element to your salads.

Tempeh: Fermented soybeans form the base for tempeh, which can be sliced or crumbled and added to salads for a protein-packed, plant-based option.

Edamame: Immature soybeans, edamame can be boiled or steamed and tossed into salads for a vibrant, high-protein addition.

Quinoa: A gluten-free pseudo-grain, quinoa is a complete protein source that can be cooked and added to salads for added texture and nutrition.

Chia Seeds: Small but mighty, chia seeds can be sprinkled onto salads for a protein and fiber boost.

Green Peas: Fresh or frozen, green peas can be quickly cooked and added to salads for a pop of color, flavor, and protein.

Seitan: Made from wheat gluten, seitan is a high-protein, plant-based option that can be sliced or cubed and incorporated into salads for a meaty texture.

25 SALADS 40G+ PROTEIN

CHICKEN AND QUINOA SALAD

INGREDIENTS

- 1 cup uncooked quinoa
- 2 cups water
- 1¾ lb. boneless, skinless chicken breasts
- Salt and pepper, to taste
- 2 cups baby spinach
- 1 cup cherry tomatoes, halved
- 1 cup cooked black beans or canned, drained, and rinsed
- ¼ cup chopped red onion

Avocado Dressing:
- 1 ripe avocado
- ¼ cup fresh cilantro
- ¼ cup plain Greek yogurt
- ¼ cup olive oil
- Juice of 1 lime
- 1 garlic clove
- Salt and pepper, to taste

 Prep Time: 20   Cook Time: 20   Servings: 4

Nutrition
Calories: 580, Protein: 42g, Fat: 25g, Carbs: 50g

PREPARATION

1. Rinse quinoa under cold water and cook according to package instructions. Set aside to cool. Season chicken breasts with salt and pepper. Grill or pan-sear over medium heat until cooked through, about 6-8 minutes per side. Rest for 5 minutes, then cut into strips.
2. In the food blender, combine all dressing ingredients and blend until smooth. Season with salt and pepper to taste.
3. Combine cooked quinoa, spinach, cherry tomatoes, black beans, and red onion in a large bowl. Add chicken strips and drizzle with avocado dressing. Toss gently to combine and serve.

STEAK AND SPINACH SALAD WITH CHEESE

INGREDIENTS

- 1¾ lb. sirloin steak
- Salt and pepper, to taste
- 8 cups baby spinach
- 1 cup cherry tomatoes, halved
- ½ cup crumbled blue cheese
- ¼ cup chopped red onion
- ¼ cup balsamic vinaigrette

 Prep Time: 20 Cook Time: 10 Servings: 4

Nutrition
Calories: 520, Protein: 45g, Fat: 30g, Carbs: 20g

PREPARATION

1. Season steak with salt and pepper. Grill or pan-sear over medium-high heat until the desired doneness, about 4-6 minutes for each side for medium-rare. Rest for 5 minutes, then cut into thin strips.
2. Combine spinach, cherry tomatoes, and red onion in a large bowl. Add steak strips and crumbled blue cheese. Drizzle with balsamic vinaigrette and toss gently to combine. Serve immediately.

SPICY CHICKEN AND MANGO SALAD

INGREDIENTS

- 1¾ lb. chicken breasts (without skin & bone), sliced
- 1 tbsp olive oil
- 1 tsp chili powder
- ½ tsp cumin
- ½ tsp paprika
- Salt and pepper, to taste
- 2 cups mixed greens
- 1 mango, peeled and sliced
- ¼ cup diced red onion
- ¼ cup chopped fresh cilantro
- ¼ cup crumbled feta cheese

Lime-Cilantro Vinaigrette:
- ¼ cup fresh lime juice
- ¼ cup olive oil
- 1 garlic clove, minced
- 2 tbsp chopped fresh cilantro
- 1 tsp honey
- Salt and crushed pepper, to taste

 Prep Time: 20　 Cook Time: 10　 Servings: 4

Nutrition
Calories: 365, Protein: 42g, Fat: 13g, Carbs: 20g

PREPARATION

1. Heat one tbsp oil in a non-stick skillet over medium-high heat. Season sliced chicken with chili powder, cumin, paprika, salt, and pepper. Sear for 3-4 minutes for each side until browned and cooked. Let cool.
2. In a small bowl, whisk together lime-cilantro vinaigrette ingredients. Combine mixed greens, sliced mango, diced red onion, chopped fresh cilantro, and cooled sliced chicken in a large bowl. Drizzle with lime-cilantro vinaigrette and toss gently to combine. Sprinkle with crumbled feta cheese and serve.

GRILLED SHRIMP AND ASPARAGUS SALAD

INGREDIENTS

- 2 lb. large shrimp, peeled and deveined
- 1 lb. asparagus, trimmed
- Olive oil for brushing
- Salt and pepper, to taste
- 8 cups mixed greens
- ½ cup cherry tomatoes, halved
- ¼ cup crumbled feta cheese
- ¼ cup sliced almonds

Lemon Vinaigrette:
- 1/4 cup olive oil
- Juice of 1 lemon
- 2 tbsp white wine vinegar
- 1 garlic clove, minced
- Salt and pepper, to taste

 Prep Time: 20 Cook Time: 10 Servings: 4

Nutrition
Calories: 420, Protein: 45g, Fat: 20g, Carbs: 20g

PREPARATION

1. Preheat the grill to medium-high heat. Brush shrimp and asparagus with olive oil and season with salt and pepper. Grill shrimp for 2-3 minutes per side until opaque and cooked. Grill asparagus for 4-6 minutes, turning occasionally, until tender and slightly charred.
2. Cut asparagus into 1-inch pieces. In a bowl, whisk the vinaigrette ingredients. Combine mixed greens, cherry tomatoes, grilled shrimp, and asparagus in a large bowl. Drizzle with lemon vinaigrette and toss to combine.
3. Top with crumbled feta cheese and sliced almonds before serving.

TUNA AND WHITE BEAN SALAD WITH PESTO

INGREDIENTS

- 3 cans (5 oz. each) of solid white albacore tuna, drained
- 1 can (15 oz.) cannellini beans, drained and rinsed
- 2 cups arugula
- 1 cup cherry tomatoes, halved
- ½ cup chopped cucumber
- ¼ cup thinly sliced red onion
- ¼ cup prepared pesto
- Salt and pepper, to taste

 Prep Time: 15   Cook Time: 00   Servings:

Nutrition
Calories: 420, Protein: 45g, Fat: 20g, Carbs: 20g

PREPARATION

1. Gently mix the tuna, cannellini beans, arugula, cherry tomatoes, cucumber, and red onion in a bowl.
2. Add pesto and gently toss to coat the salad evenly. Add salt and crushed pepper to taste. Divide salad among 4 plates and serve immediately and enjoy.

THAI TURKEY SALAD WITH PEANUT DRESSING

INGREDIENTS

- 1¾ lb. ground turkey
- 1 tbsp olive oil
- Salt and pepper, to taste
- 8 cups mixed greens
- 1 cup shredded carrots
- 1 cup bean sprouts
- ½ cup thinly sliced red bell pepper
- ¼ cup chopped green onions
- ¼ cup chopped fresh cilantro

Peanut Dressing:
- ¼ cup creamy peanut butter
- 2 tbsp soy sauce
- 2 tbsp rice vinegar
- 1 tbsp honey
- 1 tsp sesame oil
- 1 tsp grated fresh ginger
- 1 garlic clove, minced
- 2-3 tbsp water, to thin

 Prep Time: 20 Cook Time: 15 Servings: 4

Nutrition
Calories: 530, Protein: 45g, Fat: 25g, Carbs: 35g

PREPARATION

1. In a non-stick skillet, heat one tbsp of oil over medium heat. Add ground turkey, salt, and crushed pepper, and cook until browned and cooked for 7-10 minutes. Set aside to cool. In a small bowl, whisk together peanut dressing ingredients until smooth.
2. Adjust consistency with water as needed. Combine mixed greens, carrots, bean sprouts, red bell pepper, green onions, and cilantro in a bowl. Add cooked turkey and drizzle with peanut dressing. Toss gently to combine and serve.

SMOKY CHICKEN, SWEET POTATO & BEAN SALAD

INGREDIENTS

- 1¾ lb. chicken breasts without skin & bone
- 2 medium sweet potatoes, peeled and diced
- 1 tbsp olive oil
- 1 tsp smoked paprika
- Salt and pepper, to taste
- 1 can (15 oz weight) black beans, drained and rinsed
- 6 cups chopped kale; stems removed
- ½ cup cherry tomatoes, halved
- ¼ cup thinly sliced red onion
- 1 avocado, sliced

Smoky Vinaigrette:
- ¼ cup olive oil
- 2 tbsp apple cider vinegar
- 1 tbsp honey
- 1 tsp smoked paprika
- 1 garlic clove, minced
- Salt and pepper, to taste

 Prep Time: 25 Cook Time: 25 Servings: 4

Nutrition
Calories: 500, Protein: 40g, Fat: 20g, Carbs: 50g

PREPARATION

1. Set the oven heat to 400°F. Toss sweet potatoes with olive oil, smoked paprika, salt, and pepper, and spread on a baking sheet. Roast for 27-30 minutes until tender and slightly browned. Set aside to cool.
2. Season chicken breasts with salt and pepper. Grill or pan-sear over medium heat until cooked through, about 6-8 minutes per side. Rest for 5 minutes, then make the strips with a sharp knife.
3. In a bowl, whisk the smoky vinaigrette ingredients. In a bowl, add chopped kale and massage with 2 tbsp of the vinaigrette to soften the leaves. Add cherry tomatoes, red onion, black beans, and roasted sweet potatoes. Toss to combine.
4. Divide the kale mixture among 4 plates. Top with sliced chicken and avocado. Drizzle with the remaining smoky vinaigrette and serve.

GREEK SALAD WITH GRILLED CHICKEN AND FETA

INGREDIENTS

- 1¾ lb. chicken breasts without skin & bone
- Salt and pepper, to taste
- 8 cups mixed greens
- 1 cup cherry tomatoes, halved
- 1 cup sliced cucumber
- ½ cup Kalamata olives, pitted
- ½ cup crumbled feta cheese
- ¼ cup thinly sliced red onion

Greek Dressing:
- ¼ cup olive oil
- 2 tbsp red wine vinegar
- 1 tsp dried oregano
- 1 garlic clove, minced
- Salt and pepper, to taste

 Prep Time: 20   Cook Time: 20   Servings: 4

Nutrition
Calories: 510, Protein: 45g, Fat: 28g, Carbs: 20g

PREPARATION

1. Season chicken breasts with salt and crushed pepper. Grill or pan-sear over medium heat until cooked through, about 6-8 minutes per side. Rest for 4-5 minutes, then cut into strips with a sharp knife. In a bowl, whisk the Greek dressing ingredients.
2. Combine mixed greens with cherry tomatoes, cucumber, olives, and red onion in a bowl. Add chicken strips, crumbled feta cheese, and drizzle with Greek dressing. Toss gently to combine and serve.

SALMON AND FARRO SALAD WITH DILL-YOGURT DRESSING

INGREDIENTS

- 1 cup uncooked farro
- 2 cups water
- 1¾ lb. salmon fillet
- Salt and pepper, to taste
- Olive oil for brushing
- 8 cups mixed greens
- 1 cup cherry tomatoes, halved
- ½ cup thinly sliced cucumber
- ¼ cup chopped red onion

Dill-Yogurt Dressing:
- 1 cup plain Greek yogurt
- ¼ cup chopped fresh dill
- 2 tbsp lemon juice
- 1 garlic clove, minced
- Salt and crushed pepper, to taste

 Prep Time: 20 Cook Time: 25 Servings: 4

Nutrition
Calories: 550, Protein: 42g, Fat: 25g, Carbs: 45g

PREPARATION

1. Prepare farro as directed to package instructions in 2 cups of water. Set aside to cool. Put the non-stick pan over medium-high heat. Brush salmon with olive oil and powder with salt and crushed pepper. Cook 4-6 minutes for each side until cooked through and flake easily with a fork.
2. Let cool, then flake into bite-sized pieces. In a bowl, whisk the dill-yogurt dressing ingredients. Combine mixed greens with cherry tomatoes, cucumber, and red onion in a bowl. Add cooked farro and flaked salmon, then drizzle with dill-yogurt dressing. Toss gently to combine and serve.

SPICY TOFU AND EDAMAME SALAD

INGREDIENTS

- 2 lb. extra-firm tofu, pressed and cubed
- 2 tbsp vegetable oil
- 2 tbsp soy sauce
- 1 tbsp Sriracha or chili garlic sauce
- 2 cups shelled edamame, cooked
- 8 cups mixed greens
- 1 cup shredded carrots
- ½ cup thinly sliced red bell pepper

Sesame-Ginger Dressing:

- ¼ cup soy sauce
- 2 tbsp rice vinegar
- 2 tbsp sesame oil
- 1 tbsp honey
- 1 tbsp grated fresh ginger
- 1 garlic clove, minced

 Prep Time: 20 Cook Time: 10 Servings: 4

Nutrition
Calories: 430, Protein: 40g, Fat: 20g, Carbs: 30g

PREPARATION

1. In a skillet, heat two tbsp oil over medium heat. Add tofu and cook until browned on all sides, about 8-10 minutes. In a bowl, whisk soy sauce and Sriracha or chili garlic sauce. Pour the mixture over the cooked tofu, stirring gently to coat. Set aside to cool.
2. In a bowl, whisk sesame-ginger dressing ingredients. Combine mixed greens, edamame, shredded carrots, and red bell pepper in a bowl. Add spicy tofu and drizzle with sesame-ginger dressing. Toss gently to combine and serve.

MEDITERRANEAN CHICKEN SALAD WITH GRILLED HALLOUMI

INGREDIENTS

- 2 cans (15 oz. each weight) of chickpeas, drained and rinsed
- 1 cup cherry tomatoes, halved
- 1 cup diced cucumber
- ½ cup thinly sliced red onion
- ½ cup chopped fresh parsley
- ¼ cup chopped fresh mint
- 8 oz. halloumi cheese, sliced
- 1¾ lb. chicken breasts without skin & bone
- Olive oil for brushing
- Salt and pepper, to taste

Lemon Vinaigrette:
- ¼ cup olive oil
- Juice of 1 lemon
- 1 garlic clove, minced
- Salt and crushed pepper, to taste

 Prep Time: 25 Cook Time: 15 Servings: 4

Nutrition
Calories: 620, Protein: 45g, Fat: 28g, Carbs: 50g

PREPARATION

1. Combine chickpeas with cherry tomatoes, cucumber, red onion, parsley, and mint in a bowl. In a bowl, whisk the lemon vinaigrette ingredients. Preheat the grill pan to medium-high heat. Brush halloumi slices and chicken breasts with olive oil and season with salt and pepper.
2. Grill halloumi for 2-3 minutes per side until golden brown and slightly charred. Grill chicken breasts for 6-8 minutes per side until cooked through. Rest the chicken for 5 minutes, then make the slice. Drizzle lemon vinaigrette over the chickpea mixture and toss gently to combine.
3. Serve topped with grilled halloumi slices and sliced chicken.

SHRIMP AND QUINOA SALAD

INGREDIENTS

- 1 cup uncooked quinoa
- 2 cups water
- 2 lbs. large shrimp, peeled and deveined
- Olive oil for brushing
- Salt and crushed pepper, to taste
- 1 cup cherry tomatoes, halved
- 1 cup diced cucumber
- ¾ cup crumbled feta cheese
- ¼ cup chopped fresh mint
- ¼ cup chopped fresh parsley

Lemon Vinaigrette:
- ¼ cup olive oil
- Juice of 1 lemon
- 1 garlic clove, minced
- Salt and pepper, to taste

 Prep Time: 20 Cook Time: 20 Servings: 4

Nutrition
Calories: 580, Protein: 45g, Fat: 20g, Carbs: 50g

PREPARATION

1. Prepare quinoa as directed by packet instructions in 2 cups of water. Set aside to cool. Preheat a grill to medium-high heat. Brush shrimp with olive oil and add salt and pepper. Grill shrimp for 2-3 minutes for each side until pink and cooked thoroughly.
2. Combine a bowl of cooled quinoa with cherry tomatoes, cucumber, feta cheese, mint, and parsley. Add grilled shrimp and drizzle with lemon vinaigrette. Toss gently to combine and serve.

BAKED BEEF SALAD WITH SLICED AVOCADO AND TOMATO

INGREDIENTS

- 1½ lb. lean beef steak, thinly sliced (for extra protein, use a high-protein beef cut)
- 2 large ripe avocados, sliced
- 4 medium tomatoes, sliced
- 8 cups mixed greens (baby spinach, arugula, and romaine)
- ½ cup chopped red onion
- ¼ cup chopped fresh cilantro
- ¼ cup olive oil
- ¼ cup lime juice
- 1 tsp ground cumin
- Salt and pepper, to taste

 Prep Time: 20   Cook Time: 20   Servings: 4

Nutrition
Calories: 562, Protein: 43g, Fat: 35g, Carbs: 20g

PREPARATION

1. Set the oven heat to 400°F (200°C). Season the beef slices with salt and crushed pepper and put them on the baking sheet lined with parchment paper. Bake the beef slices for 17-20 minutes. Remove from the oven and put them aside to rest for 2-3 minutes.
2. Combine mixed greens, sliced avocado, sliced tomatoes, chopped red onion, and chopped cilantro in a bowl. Whisk the olive oil, lime juice, ground cumin, salt, and crushed pepper to make the dressing.
3. Drizzle the lemon oil dressing over the salad and toss to combine. Top the salad with the baked beef slices and serve immediately.

STEAK AND ARUGULA SALAD WITH GOAT CHEESE

INGREDIENTS

- 1¾ lb. sirloin steak, trimmed
- Salt and pepper, to taste
- Olive oil for brushing
- 6 cups arugula
- 1 cup cooked quinoa, cooled
- ½ cup crumbled goat cheese
- ½ cup chopped walnuts, toasted
- ½ cup thinly sliced red onion

Balsamic Vinaigrette:

- ¼ cup olive oil
- 3 tbsp balsamic vinegar
- 1 garlic clove, minced
- Salt and pepper, to taste

 Prep Time: 25 Cook Time: 15 Servings: 4

┌─ **Nutrition** ─
: Calories: 650, Protein: 45g, Fat: 30g, Carbs: 50g

PREPARATION

1. Preheat a grill to medium-high heat. Powder steak with salt and pepper, and brush with olive oil. Grill steak for 5-7 minutes for each side or until the desired doneness is reached. Put aside for 5 minutes, then chop against the grain.
2. In a bowl, whisk the balsamic vinaigrette ingredients. Combine arugula, quinoa, goat cheese, walnuts, and red onion in a bowl. Add sliced steak and drizzle with balsamic vinaigrette. Toss gently to combine and serve.

CHICKEN AND MOZZARELLA SALAD

INGREDIENTS

- 1¾ lb. boneless, skinless chicken breasts
- Salt and crushed pepper, to taste
- Olive oil for brushing
- ¼ cup prepared pesto
- 6 cups mixed greens
- 1 cup cherry tomatoes, halved
- ½ cup thinly sliced red onion
- 1 cup pearl mozzarella balls, halved

Pesto Vinaigrette:
- ¼ cup prepared pesto
- 2 tbsp white wine vinegar
- ¼ cup olive oil
- Salt and pepper, to taste

 Prep Time: 20 Cook Time: 15 Servings: 4

Nutrition
Calories: 610, Protein: 45g, Fat: 30g, Carbs: 40g

PREPARATION

1. Preheat a grill to medium-high heat. Powder chicken breasts with salt and crushed pepper, and brush with olive oil. Grill the breasts for 6-8 minutes per side until cooked thoroughly. Let rest for 5 minutes, then slice.
2. In a bowl, whisk the pesto vinaigrette ingredients. Combine mixed greens, cherry tomatoes, red onion, and mozzarella balls in a bowl. Add sliced chicken and drizzle with pesto vinaigrette. Toss gently to combine and serve.

TURKEY, QUINOA, AND CRANBERRIES SALAD

INGREDIENTS

- 1 cup uncooked quinoa
- 2 cups water
- 1¾ lb. cooked turkey breast, diced
- 1 cup dried cranberries
- 1 cup chopped pecans, toasted
- ½ cup chopped green onions
- ½ cup chopped fresh parsley

Apple Cider Vinaigrette:

- ¼ cup olive oil
- 3 tbsp apple cider vinegar
- 1 tbsp honey
- Salt and crushed pepper, to taste

 Prep Time: 20 Cook Time: 20 Servings: 4

Nutrition
Calories: 600, Protein: 42g, Fat: 27g, Carbs: 50g

PREPARATION

1. Prepare the quinoa as directed by packet instructions in 2 cups of water. Set aside to cool. Combine a bowl of cooled quinoa, diced turkey, cranberries, pecans, green onions, and parsley. In a bowl, whisk the apple cider vinaigrette ingredients.
2. Drizzle vinaigrette over the salad and toss gently to combine. Serve chilled, and enjoy.

SMOKED SALMON AND BEET SALAD

INGREDIENTS

-
- 1¾ lb. smoked salmon, sliced
- 4 cups mixed greens
- 2 cups cooked beets, sliced
- ½ cup thinly sliced red onion
- ¼ cup capers drained
- 4 oz. goat cheese, crumbled

Horseradish Dressing:
- ¼ cup olive oil
- 2 tbsp lemon juice
- 2 tbsp prepared horseradish
- 1 garlic clove, minced
- Salt and pepper, to taste

 Prep Time: 20   Cook Time: 00   Servings: 4

Nutrition
Calories: 480, Protein: 42g, Fat: 24g, Carbs: 30g

PREPARATION

1. Combine mixed greens with beets, red onion, and capers in a bowl. In a bowl, whisk the horseradish dressing ingredients.
2. Arrange salad on plates, top the salad bed with smoked salmon and crumbled goat cheese, then drizzle with horseradish dressing. Toss well, serve immediately, and enjoy.

TOFU AND BROCCOLI SALAD WITH PEANUT DRESSING

INGREDIENTS

- ¼ cup sesame seeds
- 4 cups broccoli florets
- 3 lb. extra-firm tofu, drained and cubed
- Olive oil for brushing
- Salt and pepper, to taste
- 4 cups mixed greens
- Peanut Dressing:
- ¼ cup smooth peanut butter
- 2 tbsp soy sauce
- 2 tbsp rice vinegar
- 1 tbsp honey
- 1 tsp grated ginger
- 1 garlic clove, minced
- ¼ cup water

 Prep Time: 20   Cook Time: 15   Servings: 4

Nutrition
Calories: 620, Protein: 45g, Fat: 38g, Carbs: 40g

PREPARATION

1. Set the oven to 400°F. Arrange the baking sheet with parchment paper. Toss tofu cubes with sesame seeds, brush with olive oil, and powder with salt and crushed pepper. Arrange on the sheet and bake for 13-15 minutes; flip until golden and crisp after halftime.
2. While tofu bakes, steam broccoli florets until tender-crisp, about 5 minutes. Rinse with cold water over the cooking process and set aside. In a small bowl, whisk together peanut dressing ingredients. If the dressing looks thick, add more water to achieve desired consistency.
3. Combine mixed greens, steamed broccoli, and baked sesame tofu in a large bowl. Drizzle with peanut dressing and toss gently to combine. Serve immediately.

TUNA AND CORN SALAD

INGREDIENTS

- 3 cans (5 oz each) solid white tuna in water, drained and flaked
- 1 can (15 oz) sweet corn, drained
- 1 cup cooked quinoa
- ½ cup red onion, finely chopped
- ½ cup cherry tomatoes, halved
- ¼ cup chopped fresh parsley
- ¼ cup chopped fresh cilantro
- ¼ cup freshly squeezed lemon juice
- ¼ cup olive oil
- Salt and crushed pepper, to taste

 Prep Time: 15   Cook Time: 0   Servings: 4

Nutrition
Calories: 435, Protein: 42g, Fat: 19g, Carbs: 28g

PREPARATION

1. Combine the drained and flaked tuna, drained corn, cooked quinoa, chopped red onion, cherry tomatoes, chopped parsley, and chopped cilantro in a bowl. Whisk the olive oil with lemon juice, salt, and crushed pepper to create the dressing.
2. Pour the dressing over the tuna corn salad and mix well to combine. Refrigerate for thirty minutes to allow the flavors to meld. Serve chilled, garnished with extra parsley and cilantro if desired.

SHRIMP AND AVOCADO SALAD

INGREDIENTS

- 2 lbs. large shrimp, peeled and deveined
- Olive oil for brushing
- Salt and pepper, to taste
- 2 avocados, diced
- 1 cup cherry tomatoes, halved
- ½ cup thinly sliced red onion
- ¼ cup chopped fresh cilantro
- 6 cups mixed greens

Lime-Cilantro Dressing:
- ¼ cup olive oil
- ¼ cup fresh lime juice
- ¼ cup chopped fresh cilantro
- 1 garlic clove, minced
- Salt and crushed pepper, to taste

 Prep Time: 15 Cook Time: 05 Servings: 4

Nutrition
Calories: 480, Protein: 45g, Fat: 24g, Carbs: 30g

PREPARATION

1. Preheat a grill pan to medium-high heat. Brush shrimp with olive oil and powder with salt and crushed pepper. Grill shrimp for 2-3 minutes per side until pink and cooked thoroughly. In a bowl, whisk the lime-cilantro dressing ingredients.
2. Combine mixed greens with avocado, cherry tomatoes, red onion, and chopped cilantro. Add grilled shrimp and drizzle with a lime-cilantro dressing. Toss gently to combine and serve.

CHICKEN, STRAWBERRY, AND SPINACH SALAD

INGREDIENTS

- 1¾ lb. boneless, skinless chicken breasts
- Olive oil for brushing
- Salt and pepper, to taste
- 6 cups baby spinach
- 2 cups sliced strawberries
- ½ cup thinly sliced red onion
- ½ cup crumbled feta cheese
- ½ cup chopped walnuts, toasted

Poppy Seed Dressing:
- ¼ cup olive oil
- 2 tbsp white wine vinegar
- 2 tbsp honey
- 1 tbsp poppy seeds
- Salt and crushed pepper, to taste

 Prep Time: 20   Cook Time: 15   Servings: 4

Nutrition
Calories: 580, Protein: 43g, Fat: 28g, Carbs: 40g

PREPARATION

1. Preheat a grill pan to medium-high heat. Brush chicken breasts with olive oil and powder with salt and pepper. Grill chicken for 6-8 minutes for each side until cooked through. Put it aside to rest for 5 minutes, then slice.
2. In a bowl, whisk the poppy seed dressing ingredients. Combine baby spinach, strawberries, red onion, feta cheese, and walnuts in a bowl. Add sliced chicken and drizzle with poppy seed dressing. Toss gently to combine and serve.

GRILLED PORK AND NECTARINE SALAD

INGREDIENTS

- 1¾ lb. pork tenderloin, trimmed
- Olive oil for brushing
- Salt and pepper, to taste
- 4 ripe nectarines, halved and pitted
- 6 cups mixed greens
- ½ cup crumbled goat cheese
- ½ cup chopped almonds, toasted

Honey-Balsamic Vinaigrette:
- ¼ cup olive oil
- 3 tbsp balsamic vinegar
- 2 tbsp honey
- Salt and crushed pepper, to taste

 Prep Time: 20 Cook Time: 15 Servings: 4

Nutrition
Calories: 600, Protein: 42g, Fat: 30g, Carbs: 45g

PREPARATION

1. Preheat a grill pan to medium-high heat. Brush pork tenderloin and nectarine halves with olive oil and powder with salt and crushed pepper. Grill pork for 5-7 minutes for each side or until the desired doneness is reached.
2. Grill nectarines for 2-3 minutes per side until grill marks appear and they are slightly softened. Let pork rest for 5 minutes, then slice. Cut nectarines into wedges. In a bowl, whisk the honey-balsamic vinaigrette ingredients.
3. Combine mixed greens, grilled nectarine wedges, goat cheese, and almonds in a large bowl. Add sliced pork and drizzle with honey-balsamic vinaigrette. Toss gently to combine and serve.

SEARED SCALLOPS AND GRAPEFRUIT SALAD

INGREDIENTS

- 2 lb. large sea scallops, patted dry
- Olive oil for brushing
- Salt and crushed pepper, to taste
- 2 large grapefruits, peeled and sectioned
- 6 cups mixed greens
- ¼ cup thinly sliced red onion
- ¼ cup chopped fresh mint
- ½ cup crumbled feta cheese

Citrus Vinaigrette:
- ¼ cup olive oil
- 3 tbsp fresh grapefruit juice
- 1 tbsp fresh lemon juice
- 1 tbsp honey
- Salt and pepper, to taste

 Prep Time: 20 Cook Time: 05 Servings: 4

Nutrition
Calories: 480, Protein: 40g, Fat: 24g, Carbs: 30g

PREPARATION

1. Put the non-stick skillet over medium-high heat. Brush scallops with olive oil and powder with salt and crushed pepper. Sear scallops for 2-3 minutes per side until golden brown and cooked through. Remove from heat and set aside.
2. In a bowl, whisk the citrus vinaigrette ingredients. Combine mixed greens with grapefruit sections, red onion, mint, and feta cheese in a bowl. Add seared scallops and drizzle with citrus vinaigrette. Toss gently to combine and serve.

BUFFALO CHICKEN AND BLUE CHEESE SALAD

INGREDIENTS

- 1¾ lb. chicken breasts (without skin & bone)
- ½ cup buffalo wing sauce
- Olive oil for brushing
- Salt and pepper, to taste
- 6 cups chopped romaine lettuce
- 1 cup thinly sliced celery
- 1 cup shredded carrots
- ½ cup crumbled blue cheese

Ranch Dressing:
- ½ cup buttermilk
- ¼ cup mayonnaise
- ¼ cup sour cream
- 1 tbsp chopped fresh chives
- ½ tsp garlic powder
- ½ tsp onion powder
- Salt and pepper, to taste

 Prep Time: 20   Cook Time: 15   Servings: 4

Nutrition
Calories: 640, Protein: 46g, Fat: 34g, Carbs: 35g

PREPARATION

1. Preheat a grill pan to medium-high heat. Brush chicken breasts with olive oil and powder with salt and pepper. Grill chicken for 6-8 minutes for each side until cooked thoroughly. Remove from heat and put it aside for 5 minutes. Slice chicken and toss with buffalo wing sauce.
2. In a bowl, whisk the ranch dressing ingredients. In a bowl, combine chopped romaine lettuce, celery, and carrots. Topped with buffalo chicken and crumbled blue cheese. Drizzle with ranch dressing and serve.

TURKEY, APPLE, AND WALNUT SALAD

INGREDIENTS

- ¾ lb. cooked turkey breast, sliced
- 2 large apples, cored and thinly sliced
- ½ cup chopped walnuts, toasted
- ½ cup crumbled Gorgonzola cheese
- 6 cups mixed greens

Cranberry Vinaigrette:

- ¼ cup olive oil
- 3 tbsp cranberry juice
- 2 tbsp red wine vinegar
- 1 tbsp honey
- Salt and crushed pepper, to taste

 Prep Time: 20 Cook Time: 00 Servings: 4

Nutrition
Calories: 640, Protein: 46g, Fat: 34g, Carbs: 35g

PREPARATION

1. In a bowl, whisk the cranberry vinaigrette ingredients. Combine mixed greens with sliced apples, walnuts, and Gorgonzola cheese in a bowl. Add sliced turkey and drizzle with cranberry vinaigrette. Toss gently to combine and serve.

25 SALADS. 25G+ PROTEIN

THAI BEEF SALAD WITH CILANTRO AND LIME

INGREDIENTS

- 1 lb. flank steak
- Salt and crushed pepper, to taste
- 6 cups mixed greens
- ½ cup thinly sliced red onion
- ¼ cup chopped fresh cilantro
- ¼ cup chopped fresh mint
- ¼ cup chopped unsalted peanuts

Dressing:
- 2 tbsp fresh lime juice
- 2 tbsp olive oil
- 2 tbsp fish sauce
- 1 tbsp honey
- 1 tbsp chopped fresh ginger
- 1 garlic clove, minced
- 1 red chili pepper, seeded and minced

 Prep Time: 20   Cook Time: 10   Servings: 4

Nutrition
Calories: 315, Protein: 29g, Fat: 15g, Carbs: 16g

PREPARATION

1. Preheat a grill pan to medium-high heat. Powder the flank of the steak with salt and pepper. Grill steak for 4-5 minutes for each side until medium-rare. Put it aside for 5 minutes, then slice thinly against the grain.
2. In a bowl, whisk all the dressing elements. Combine mixed greens, red onion, cilantro, and mint in a bowl. Add sliced steak and drizzle with dressing. Toss gently to combine. Top with chopped peanuts and serve.

TOFU AND VEGETABLE POKE BOWL

INGREDIENTS

- 1 lb. extra-firm tofu, drained, pressed, and cut into 1-inch cubes
- 2 tbsp vegetable oil
- Salt and pepper, to taste
- 4 cups cooked brown rice
- 1 cup chopped cucumber
- 1 cup chopped red bell pepper
- 1 cup chopped mango
- ¼ cup chopped scallions
- ¼ cup chopped fresh cilantro
- ¼ cup chopped unsalted peanuts

Soy-Sesame Dressing:
- 3 tbsp soy sauce
- 2 tbsp rice vinegar
- 1 tbsp sesame oil
- 1 tbsp honey
- 1 tbsp grated fresh ginger
- 1 garlic clove, minced

 Prep Time: 20 Cook Time: 10 Servings: 4

Nutrition
Calories: 328, Protein: 27g, Fat: 16g, Carbs: 19g

PREPARATION

1. Heat two tbsp oil in a non-stick skillet over medium-high heat. Add tofu cubes and season with salt and pepper. Cook for 5-6 minutes; flip after some to all over or until golden brown on all sides. Remove from heat and let cool.
2. In a small bowl, whisk all the soy-sesame dressing ingredients. Combine cooked brown rice, chopped cucumber, red bell pepper, mango, scallions, and cilantro in a large bowl. Add cooked tofu and drizzle with soy-sesame dressing. Toss gently to combine.
3. Top with chopped peanuts and serve.

SHRIMP, AVOCADO, AND MANGO SALAD

INGREDIENTS

- :
- 1 lb. large shrimp, peeled and deveined
- 1 tbsp olive oil
- Salt and pepper, to taste
- 6 cups mixed greens
- 1 large ripe mango, peeled and diced
- 1 avocado, peeled, pitted, and diced
- ¼ cup chopped fresh cilantro

Honey-Lime Vinaigrette:
- 3 tbsp fresh lime juice
- 2 tbsp honey
- 1 tbsp Dijon mustard
- 1 garlic clove, minced
- 1/4 cup olive oil

 Prep Time: 20 Cook Time: 05 Servings: 4

Nutrition
Calories: 301, Protein: 26g, Fat: 13g, Carbs: 20g

PREPARATION

1. Preheat a grill pan to medium-high heat. Toss shrimp with olive oil and powder with salt and pepper. Grill shrimp for 2-3 minutes per side until cooked through. Let rest for 5 minutes, then chop. Whisk the honey-lime vinaigrette ingredients in a bowl until they are well combined.
2. Combine mixed greens, diced mango, avocado, and chopped cilantro. Add chopped shrimp and drizzle with honey-lime vinaigrette. Toss gently to combine and serve.

THAI SPICY PORK SALAD

INGREDIENTS

- 1 lb. lean pork tenderloin, thinly sliced
- ¼ cup lime juice
- 3 tbsp fish sauce
- 2 tbsp brown sugar
- 1 tsp crushed red pepper flakes
- 4 cups mixed greens
- 1 cup thinly sliced red onion
- 1 cup cherry tomatoes, halved
- ½ cup chopped fresh cilantro
- ½ cup chopped fresh mint

 Prep Time: 20 Cook Time: 10 Servings: 4

Nutrition
Calories: 410, Protein: 28g, Fat: 22g, Carbs: 26g

PREPARATION

1. Put the non-stick skillet over medium heat and cook the pork slices for 4-5 minutes for each side. Remove from heat and let cool. Whisk the lime juice, fish sauce, brown sugar, and crushed pepper flakes in a bowl to make the dressing.
2. Combine mixed greens, red onion, cherry tomatoes, cilantro, and mint in a bowl. Add cooked pork to the salad and drizzle with the dressing. Toss to combine and serve immediately.

TERIYAKI CHICKEN AND PINEAPPLE SALAD

INGREDIENTS

 Prep Time: 15 Cook Time: 20 Servings: 4

- 1 lb. chicken thighs without skin and bone
- ½ cup teriyaki sauce
- 2 cups chopped romaine lettuce
- 2 cups chopped Napa cabbage
- 1 cup diced fresh pineapple
- ¼ cup chopped green onions
- ¼ cup chopped fresh cilantro

Sesame-Ginger Dressing:
- 2 tbsp rice vinegar
- 1 tbsp soy sauce
- 1 tbsp honey
- 1 tbsp sesame oil
- 1 tbsp grated fresh ginger
- 1 garlic clove, minced

Nutrition
Calories: 360, Protein: 26g, Fat: 12g, Carbs: 36g

PREPARATION

1. Preheat the non-stick pan to medium-high heat. Brush chicken thighs with teriyaki sauce. Cook chicken for 5-6 minutes for each side until cooked through. Let rest for 5 minutes, then slice. In a bowl, whisk the sesame-ginger dressing ingredients.
2. Toss romaine lettuce, Napa cabbage, diced fresh pineapple, chopped green onions, and chopped cilantro. Add to a large bowl sliced chicken and drizzle with sesame-ginger dressing. Toss gently to combine and serve.

PAN-SEARED SALMON SALAD

INGREDIENTS

 Prep Time: 15   Cook Time: 10   Servings: 4

- 1 lb. salmon fillet, skin on
- Salt and crushed pepper, to taste
- 6 cups mixed greens
- 1 cup halved cherry tomatoes
- ¼ cup chopped fresh dill
- ¼ cup chopped red onion

Lemon-Dill Dressing:
- 2 tbsp fresh lemon juice
- 1 tbsp Dijon mustard
- 1 garlic clove, minced
- ¼ cup olive oil
- Salt and pepper, to taste

Nutrition
: Calories: 280, Protein: 25g, Fat: 17g, Carbs: 7g

PREPARATION

1. Heat a non-stick skillet over medium-high heat. Powder salmon fillet with salt and pepper. Place skin side down in the skillet and cook for 5-6 minutes until golden and crispy. Carefully flip the salmon and cook for 3-4 minutes until cooked.
2. Remove from heat and let cool. In a bowl, whisk the lemon-dill dressing ingredients. Combine mixed greens with halved cherry tomatoes, chopped fresh dill, and chopped red onion in a bowl. Flake cooked salmon over the top and drizzle with lemon-dill dressing.
3. Toss gently to combine and serve.

CURRIED CHICKEN SALAD

INGREDIENTS

- 4 cups cooked and shredded chicken breast
- 1 cup chopped celery
- ½ cup diced red onion
- ½ cup raisins
- ½ cup chopped almonds
- ½ cup plain Greek yogurt
- ¼ cup mayonnaise
- 2 tbsp curry powder
- Salt and pepper, to taste

 Prep Time: 20 Cook Time: 00 Servings: 4

Nutrition
Calories: 450, Protein: 29g, Fat: 28g, Carbs: 20g

PREPARATION

1. Combine chicken, celery, red onion, raisins, and almonds in a bowl. Whisk the Greek yogurt with mayonnaise, curry powder, salt, and pepper in a bowl. Pour the yogurt mayonnaise dressing over the chicken mixture and mix well to combine.
2. Serve chilled over a bed of mixed greens or on whole-grain bread.

MEDITERRANEAN TUNA SALAD WITH OLIVES & ARTICHOKES

INGREDIENTS

- 2 cans (5 oz.) tuna in water, drained
- 6 cups mixed greens
- ¾ cup halved cherry tomatoes
- ¾ cup sliced cucumber
- ½ cup chopped Kalamata olives
- ½ cup chopped marinated artichoke hearts

Lemon-Dijon Dressing:
- 2 tbsp fresh lemon juice
- 1 tbsp Dijon mustard
- 1 garlic clove, minced
- ¼ cup olive oil
- Salt and pepper, to taste

 Prep Time: 10   Cook Time: 05   Servings: 4

Nutrition
Calories: 321, Protein: 26g, Fat: 17g, Carbs: 16g

PREPARATION

1. In a bowl, whisk the lemon-Dijon dressing ingredients. Combine drained tuna, mixed greens, halved cherry tomatoes, sliced cucumber, chopped Kalamata olives, and chopped marinated artichoke hearts in a bowl. Drizzle with lemon-Dijon dressing and toss gently to combine. Serve

EGGPLANT AND CHICKPEA SALAD WITH POMEGRANATE MOLASSES

INGREDIENTS

- 1 large eggplant, cut into 1-inch cubes
- 1 tbsp olive oil
- Salt and crushed pepper, to taste
- 2 cans (15 oz weight) chickpeas, drained and rinsed
- 2 cups crumbled feta cheese
- 6 cups mixed greens
- ¼ cup chopped fresh parsley
- Pomegranate Molasses
  Dressing:
- 2 tbsp pomegranate molasses
- 1 tbsp red wine vinegar
- 1 tbsp honey
- ¼ cup olive oil
- Salt and pepper, to taste

 Prep Time: 20 Cook Time: 10 Servings: 4

Nutrition
Calories: 400, Protein: 26g, Fat: 20g, Carbs: 29g

PREPARATION

1. Preheat a grill pan to medium-high heat. Toss eggplant cubes with olive oil and season with salt and pepper. Grill eggplant for 3-4 minutes for each side until tender and charred. Remove from heat and let cool.
2. In a bowl, whisk the pomegranate molasses dressing ingredients. Combine cooked eggplant cubes, drained and rinsed chickpeas, mixed greens, crumbled feta cheese, and chopped fresh parsley in a bowl. Drizzle with pomegranate molasses dressing and toss gently to combine. Serve.

BEEF TACO SALAD

INGREDIENTS

- 1 lb. lean ground beef
- 1 packet taco seasoning
- ¼ cup water
- 8 cups chopped romaine lettuce
- 1 cup cherry tomatoes, halved
- 1 cup canned black beans, drained, and rinsed
- 1 cup shredded cheddar cheese
- ½ cup chopped green onions
- ½ cup chopped cilantro
- ½ cup salsa
- ½ cup sour cream
- 1 avocado, diced

 Prep Time: 10   Cook Time: 20   Servings: 4

Nutrition
Calories: 520, Protein: 30g, Fat: 30g, Carbs: 34g

PREPARATION

1. In a non-stick skillet, cook ground beef over medium heat until browned. Drain excess fat. Add taco seasoning with water to the skillet, stir well, and simmer for 5 minutes. Combine romaine lettuce with cherry tomatoes, black beans, cheddar cheese, green onions, and cilantro in a bowl.
2. Top the salad with the cooked ground beef, salsa, sour cream, and diced avocado. Toss to combine and serve immediately.

TUNA AND ORZO SALAD WITH LEMON-CAPER DRESSING

INGREDIENTS

- 1 lb. orzo pasta
- 2 cans (5 oz weight) tuna in water, drained
- 2 cups chopped arugula
- ½ cup chopped sun-dried tomatoes
- ¼ cup chopped capers
- ¼ cup chopped fresh parsley

Lemon-Caper Dressing:

- ¼ cup olive oil
- 2 tbsp fresh lemon juice
- 1 garlic clove, minced
- 1 tbsp chopped capers
- Salt and pepper, to taste

 Prep Time: 10 Cook Time: 10 Servings: 4

Nutrition

Calories: 320, Protein: 25g, Fat: 12g, Carbs: 27g

PREPARATION

1. Prepare the orzo pasta as directed to packet instructions until al dente. Drain and rinse with cold water. In a bowl, whisk the lemon-caper dressing ingredients. Combine cooked orzo pasta, drained tuna, chopped arugula, sun-dried tomatoes, chopped capers, and chopped fresh parsley in a bowl.
2. Drizzle with lemon-caper dressing and toss gently to combine. Serve.

SOUTHWESTERN QUINOA AND BLACK BEAN SALAD

INGREDIENTS

- 1½ cup quinoa, rinsed and drained
- 2 cans (15 oz weight) of black beans, drained and rinsed
- 1 cup frozen corn kernels, thawed
- ½ cup diced red onion
- ¼ cup chopped fresh cilantro
- ½ cup shredded cheese (any you like)

Lime-Cumin Vinaigrette:
- ¼ cup olive oil
- 2 tbsp fresh lime juice
- 1 garlic clove, minced
- 1 tsp ground cumin
- Salt and pepper, to taste

 Prep Time: 10 Cook Time: 20 Servings: 4

Nutrition
Calories: 310, Protein: 26g, Fat: 13g, Carbs: 44g

PREPARATION

1. In a saucepan, add 2 cups water, then take a boil. Add rinsed quinoa, decrease the stove heat to low, cover, and simmer for 17-20 minutes until water is absorbed and cooked thoroughly. Let cool. In a bowl, whisk the lime-cumin vinaigrette ingredients.
2. Combine cooked quinoa, drained and rinsed black beans, thawed corn kernels, diced red onion, shredded cheese, and chopped fresh cilantro in a bowl. Drizzle with lime-cumin vinaigrette and toss gently to combine. Serve.

CHICKEN, PEAR, AND GORGONZOLA SALAD

INGREDIENTS

- 1 lb. chicken breasts (without skin & bone)
- 1 tbsp olive oil
- Salt and crushed pepper, to taste
- 6 cups mixed greens
- 2 pears, sliced
- ½ cup crumbled Gorgonzola cheese
- ¼ cup chopped walnuts

Honey-Mustard Dressing:
- ¼ cup Dijon mustard
- ¼ cup honey
- 2 tbsp apple cider vinegar
- ¼ cup olive oil
- Salt and pepper, to taste

 Prep Time: 10   Cook Time: 15   Servings: 4

Nutrition
Calories: 360, Protein: 26g, Fat: 18g, Carbs: 26g

PREPARATION

1. Preheat a grill pan to medium-high heat. Rub chicken breasts with olive oil and powder with salt and pepper. Grill chicken for 5-6 minutes for each side until cooked thoroughly. Let rest for 5 minutes, then slice.
2. In a bowl, whisk the honey-mustard dressing ingredients. Combine mixed greens, sliced pears, crumbled Gorgonzola cheese, chopped walnuts, and sliced grilled chicken in a large bowl. Drizzle with honey-mustard dressing and toss gently to combine. Serve.

STEAK AND ROASTED SWEET POTATO SALAD WITH CHIMICHURRI

INGREDIENTS

- 1 lb. flank steak
- 1 tbsp olive oil
- Salt and pepper, to taste
- 2 large, sweet potatoes, peeled and cubed
- 6 cups mixed greens
- ½ cup crumbled feta cheese
- ¼ cup chopped fresh parsley

Chimichurri:
- ½ cup chopped fresh parsley
- ½ cup chopped fresh cilantro
- 1 garlic clove, minced
- ¼ cup red wine vinegar
- ½ cup olive oil
- Salt and pepper, to taste

 Prep Time: 10　 Cook Time: 30　 Servings: 4

Nutrition
Calories: 400, Protein: 27g, Fat: 22g, Carbs: 26g

PREPARATION

1. Preheat oven to 400°F. Rub flank steak with olive oil and powder with salt and pepper. Roast sweet potato cubes on a baking sheet lined with parchment paper for 23-25 minutes until tender and lightly browned.
2. In a bowl, whisk the chimichurri ingredients and put them aside for later use. Combine mixed greens, crumbled feta cheese, roasted sweet potato cubes, and sliced flank steak in a bowl. Drizzle with chimichurri and toss gently to combine. Serve.

SHRIMP AND FARRO SALAD

INGREDIENTS

- 1 cup farro, rinsed and drained
- 1 lb. shrimp, peeled and deveined
- 1 fennel bulb, sliced
- 1 orange, peeled and sliced
- 4 cups baby spinach

Orange Vinaigrette:
- ¼ cup olive oil
- 2 tbsp fresh orange juice
- 1 tsp Dijon mustard
- 1 garlic clove, minced
- Salt and pepper, to taste

 Prep Time: 10 Cook Time: 20 Servings: 4

Nutrition
Calories: 380, Protein: 27g, Fat: 12g, Carbs: 41g

PREPARATION

1. In a non-stick saucepan, add 2 cups of water to a boil. Add rinsed farro, reduce heat to low, cover, and simmer for 17-20 minutes until water is absorbed and farro is tender. Let cool.
2. Heat one tbsp oil over medium-high heat in a large skillet. Add shrimp and cook for 2-3 minutes per side until pink and cooked thoroughly.
3. In a bowl, whisk the orange vinaigrette ingredients. Combine a large bowl of cooled farro, sliced fennel, sliced orange, and baby spinach. Add cooked shrimp and drizzle with orange vinaigrette. Toss gently to combine and serve.

LAMB SHAWARMA SALAD

INGREDIENTS

- 1 lb. lean lamb, thinly sliced
- 3 tbsp shawarma spice blend
- ¼ cup olive oil
- 8 cups mixed greens
- 1 cup sliced cucumber
- 1 cup cherry tomatoes, halved
- ½ cup pitted Kalamata olives
- ½ cup chopped fresh parsley
- ½ cup chopped fresh mint
- ¼ cup freshly squeezed lemon juice
- Salt and pepper, to taste

 Prep Time: 15   Cook Time: 20   Servings: 4

Nutrition
Calories: 580, Protein: 29g, Fat: 38g, Carbs: 26g

PREPARATION

1. Toss lamb with shawarma spice blend and two tbsp oil in a bowl. Marinate for thirty minutes. In a large skillet, cook the lamb slices for 4-5 minutes for each side. Remove from heat and let cool. Toss mixed greens with cucumber, tomatoes, olives, parsley, and mint in a bowl.
2. Whisk the lemon juice, leftover two tbsp oil, salt, and crushed pepper to make the dressing. Drizzle the lemon oil dressing over the salad, toss to combine, and top with the cooked lamb slices. Serve immediately.

MAYONNAISE SEAFOOD SALAD

INGREDIENTS

- 1 lb. cooked and peeled shrimp
- ½ lb. cooked and flaked crabmeat
- ½ lb. cooked and chopped squid
- 1 cup diced celery
- ½ cup diced red onion
- ½ cup chopped fresh dill
- ½ cup mayonnaise
- 2 tbsp lemon juice
- Salt and crushed pepper, to taste

 Prep Time: 10   Cook Time: 00   Servings: 4

Nutrition
Calories: 480, Protein: 32g, Fat: 28g, Carbs: 22g

PREPARATIONS

1. Toss the shrimp with crabmeat, squid, celery, red onion, and dill in a bowl. Whisk the mayonnaise, lemon juice, salt, and crushed pepper in a bowl. Pour the dressing over the seafood mixture and mix well to combine.
2. Refrigerate for at least thirty minutes to allow the flavors to meld. Serve chilled over a bed of mixed greens.

CHICKEN, BACON, AND AVOCADO SALAD

INGREDIENTS

- 1 lb. chicken breasts without skin and bone
- 4 slices bacon
- 2 avocados, sliced
- 6 cups mixed greens

Dijon Vinaigrette:

- ¼ cup olive oil
- 2 tbsp white wine vinegar
- 1 tbsp Dijon mustard
- 1 garlic clove, minced
- Salt and pepper, to taste
- Instructions:

 Prep Time: 10 Cook Time: 15 Servings: 4

Nutrition
Calories: 420, Protein: 31g, Fat: 30g, Carbs: 13g

PREPARATION

1. Preheat a grill to medium-high heat. Rub meat breasts with oil and season with salt and crushed pepper. Grill chicken for 5-6 minutes for each side until cooked thoroughly. Let rest for 5 minutes, then slice.
2. Cook bacon in a non-stick skillet over moderate heat until crisp. Let cool, then crumble. In a small bowl, whisk together Dijon vinaigrette ingredients. Combine mixed greens, sliced avocado, grilled chicken, and crumbled bacon in a bowl.
3. Drizzle with Dijon vinaigrette and toss gently to combine. Serve.

CHICKEN AND BROCCOLI SALAD

INGREDIENTS

- 2 chicken breasts (without skin and bone) (450g total)
- 360g fresh broccoli florets
- 65g dried cranberries
- 170g shredded carrot
- 1 large apple, thinly sliced
- 115g cream cheese, softened
- 50g mayonnaise
- 50g sour cream
- 20g apple cider vinegar
- Salt and crushed pepper, to taste

 Prep Time: 20   Cook Time: 20   Servings: 4

Nutrition
Calories: 456, Protein: 28g, Fat: 24g, Carbs: 32g

PREPARATION

1. **Cook the chicken breasts:** Set your oven heat to 375°F (190°C). Put the chicken breasts on the baking sheet arranged with parchment paper. Powder some salt and crushed black pepper.
2. Bake for 23-25 minutes or until cooked thoroughly. Then remove and cool for a few minutes and cut into bite-sized pieces.
3. **Blanch the broccoli:** Put the stockpot of salted water to a boil. Add the broccoli florets and cook for 1-2 minutes. Drain and immediately transfer the broccoli to a bowl of ice water. Drain again and set aside.
4. **Prepare the dressing:** In a bowl, whisk the softened cream cheese, mayonnaise, sour cream, apple cider vinegar, salt, and black pepper. Whisk until smooth and creamy.
5. In a bowl, toss the cooked chicken, blanched broccoli, dried cranberries, shredded carrot, and sliced apple. Pour the vinegar mayo dressing over the salad and toss gently until well coated. Divide the salad among four plates or bowls and enjoy!

AHI TUNA AND SPINACH SALAD

INGREDIENTS

- 1 lb. ahi tuna steaks
- 2 tbsp sesame oil
- 2 cups baby spinach
- 1 cup sliced red onion
- 1 cup shredded carrots

Ginger-Soy Dressing:
- ¼ cup low-sodium soy sauce
- 1 tbsp rice vinegar
- 2 tbsp sesame oil
- 1 garlic clove, minced
- 1 tsp grated fresh ginger

 Prep Time: 10   Cook Time: 05   Servings: 4

Nutrition
Calories: 321, Protein: 25g, Fat: 17g, Carbs: 17g

PREPARATION

1. Heat 1 tbsp oil in a non-stick skillet over medium-high heat. Powder the ahi tuna steaks with salt and crushed pepper, and sear for 2-3 minutes for each side until browned and cooked to the desired doneness. Let rest for 5 minutes, then slice.
2. In a bowl, whisk the ginger-soy dressing ingredients. Combine baby spinach, sliced red onion, and shredded carrots in a bowl. Add sliced ahi tuna and drizzle with ginger-soy dressing. Toss gently to combine and serve.

SEARED SCALLOPS AND WATERMELON SALAD

INGREDIENTS

- 1½ lb. sea scallops
- 3 tbsp olive oil
- 2 cups cubed watermelon
- ¼ cup crumbled feta cheese
- ¼ cup chopped fresh mint

Lime-Coconut Dressing:
- ¼ cup coconut milk
- 2 tbsp lime juice
- 1 tbsp honey
- 1 garlic clove, minced
- Salt and pepper, to taste

 Prep Time: 10 Cook Time: 05 Servings: 4

Nutrition
Calories: 318, Protein: 29g, Fat: 18g, Carbs: 10g

PREPARATION

1. Heat three tbsp oil in a large skillet over medium-high heat. Season sea scallops with salt and pepper, and sear for 2-3 minutes for each side until browned and cooked. Let rest for 5 minutes, then slice.
2. In a bowl, whisk the lime-coconut dressing ingredients. Combine cubed watermelon, crumbled feta cheese, chopped fresh mint, and sliced sea scallops in a bowl. Drizzle with lime-coconut dressing and toss gently to combine. Serve.

HERBED TURKEY AND FARRO SALAD

INGREDIENTS

- 1 lb. turkey breast, cooked and chopped
- 1 cup farro, cooked
- 2 cups baby spinach
- ¼ cup chopped fresh parsley
- ¼ cup chopped fresh dill

Green Goddess Dressing:

- ¼ cup mayonnaise
- ¼ cup plain Greek yogurt
- 2 tbsp chopped fresh chives
- 2 tbsp chopped fresh parsley
- 2 tbsp chopped fresh tarragon
- 1 garlic clove, minced
- 1 tbsp lemon juice
- Salt and crushed pepper, to taste

 Prep Time: 10 Cook Time: 20 Servings: 4

Nutrition
Calories: 340, Protein: 26g, Fat: 13g, Carbs: 30g

PREPARATION

1. Combine cooked farro with baby spinach, chopped fresh parsley, and chopped fresh dill in a bowl. Add chopped cooked turkey breast and drizzle with green goddess dressing. Toss gently to combine and serve.

SHRIMP AND CUCUMBER NOODLE SALAD

INGREDIENTS

- 1 lb. shrimp, peeled and deveined
- 3 tbsp olive oil
- 1 large cucumber, spiralized
- ¼ cup shredded carrots
- ¼ cup sliced red pepper

Sesame-Ginger Dressing:
- ¼ cup low-sodium soy sauce
- 1 tbsp rice vinegar
- 1 tbsp sesame oil
- 1 garlic clove, minced
- 1 tsp grated fresh ginger
- ¼ cup water

 Prep Time: 10   Cook Time: 05   Servings: 4

Nutrition
Calories: 318, Protein: 25g, Fat: 18g, Carbs: 14g

PREPARATION

1. Heat three tbsp oil in a non-stick skillet over medium-high heat. Add shrimp and cook for 2-3 minutes per side until pink and cooked through. Let cool. In a small bowl, whisk together sesame-ginger dressing ingredients.
2. Combine cucumber noodles, shredded carrots, sliced red pepper, and cooled shrimp in a large bowl. Drizzle with sesame-ginger dressing and toss gently to combine. Serve.

PINEAPPLE SHRIMP SALAD

INGREDIENTS

- 1 lb. cooked and peeled shrimp
- 2 large ripe avocados, diced
- 1 cup cherry tomatoes, halved
- 1 cup diced pineapple
- 8 cups baby spinach
- 1 large beet, peeled and thinly sliced
- ¼ cup freshly squeezed lime juice
- ¼ cup olive oil
- ¼ cup chopped fresh cilantro
- Salt and pepper, to taste

 Prep Time: 20 Cook Time: 00 Servings: 4

Nutrition
Calories: 450, Protein: 28g, Fat: 24g, Carbs: 36g

PREPARATION

1. Toss the shrimp with diced avocado, cherry tomatoes, pineapple, baby spinach, and thinly sliced beet in a bowl. Whisk the lime juice, olive oil, chopped cilantro, salt, and crushed pepper in a bowl to create the dressing.
2. Pour the dressing over the shrimp salad and toss gently to combine. Refrigerate for fifteen minutes to allow the flavors to meld. Serve chilled, garnished with extra cilantro if desired.

CONCLUSION

As we conclude "Power-Packed Salads: Fuel Your Day with Flavor and Protein", we hope that you have been inspired to embrace the world of nutritious and protein-rich salads. With 50 diverse and delicious recipes at your fingertips, we trust that this cookbook has shown you that salads can be so much more than a simple side dish. Instead, they can be the star of the meal, providing an abundance of flavors, textures, and nutrients to support your health and well-being.

Throughout this cookbook, we have endeavored to showcase a variety of ingredients and combinations to suit every taste bud, dietary preference, and nutritional need. Our selection of high-protein and moderate-protein recipes ensures that you can tailor your salad choices to your personal requirements while still enjoying mouthwatering and satisfying meals.

As you continue your culinary journey, don't hesitate to experiment with the recipes and adapt them to your liking. Swap out ingredients, try new dressings, or combine elements from different recipes to create your own unique salad masterpieces. The possibilities are truly endless.

Incorporating these power-packed salads into your daily routine will not only fuel your body with essential nutrients but also delight your palate and elevate your overall dining experience. We are confident that this cookbook has equipped you with the knowledge, inspiration, and passion to create nourishing and flavorsome salads that will quickly become staples in your meal rotation.

Thank you for joining us on this delectable adventure, and we wish you endless joy and success in the kitchen. May "Power-Packed Salads: Fuel Your Day with Flavor and Protein" be your go-to guide for crafting wholesome and scrumptious salads that truly make a difference in your health, happiness, and culinary enjoyment. Bon appétit!

Made in the USA
Las Vegas, NV
28 October 2024